PHILIP HOFER AS A COLLECTOR

A symposium in conjunction with the exhibition of the Philip Hofer bequest to the Department of Printing and Graphic Arts

THE HOUGHTON LIBRARY
HARVARD UNIVERSITY
10 NOVEMBER 1988

WILLIAM H. BOND, Librarian Emeritus
of the Houghton Library, was the moderator
of the symposium, and his comments
in italics precede the individual papers in
this booklet. The participants were William
Bentinck-Smith, Honorary Curator
of Type Specimens and Letter Design in
the Harvard College Library; Lucien
Goldschmidt; Charles Ryskamp, Director
of The Frick Collection; and Arthur Vershbow,
member of the Harvard College Library
Visiting Committee.

INTRODUCTORY REMARKS

A GREAT LIBRARY *is both luminous and numinous. It is luminous because it brings into sharp focus the brilliance of many intellects on all conceivable subjects for uses yet undreamed-of. It is numinous because it is haunted, in the best possible sense of the word, by the spirits of all those who have made its assemblage possible — writers and compilers, librarians and scholars, booksellers, bibliophiles, and benefactors, and users who have built and are building upon its foundation to advance the welfare and knowledge of mankind in ways often unimagined by their predecessors. We are surrounded by these spirits today, and the cases displayed around us here are visible, but only partial, testimony to one of the greatest. We return to the luminous: these books and manuscripts that Philip Hofer collected principally because of their visual excellence and interest are not just picture-books to look at, they shed strong and unexpected shafts of light on almost every field of the University curriculum, and they will continue to do so while still being appreciated as beautiful objects in their own right.*

Just fifty years ago the then University Librarian, Keyes DeWitt Metcalf, achieved a master-stroke by recruiting and bringing to Harvard two remarkable men: William Alexander Jackson, who within a few years became the first Librarian of the Houghton Library, as yet unbuilt; and Philip Hofer, inventor and founder of the Department of Printing and Graphic Arts, whose achievements we now salute. What they did was far greater than Keyes Metcalf can possibly have expected, and it wrought a spectacular change in what was already a magnificent library. Today we celebrate Philip Hofer's final gift to the institution he loved, and we also celebrate the tribute of admiration and love manifested by the friends of Philip Hofer in establishing the Curatorship in his name.

I leave you to imagine the extraordinary privilege I enjoyed of years spent as a friend and close colleague of two such men, each the top of his class. But I am not here to provide autobiography or history or critical judgment: the first would be inappropriate, and my four friends and colleagues on this panel will shortly deal with the other topics. William Bentinck-Smith, Philip's chosen biographer and with Mel Seiden a leader in the drive that brought the Hofer Curatorship to triumphant reality, will begin with a brief sketch of Philip's life and achievements. But before I call on him, and because his biography, "The Prince of the Eye," so far has dealt only with Phil's early life, I want to read a short poem written late in Philip's life by his nephew, Philip Heckscher. I hope that it will move you, as it does me.

My old uncle goes down slowly, fumbling for the keys.
There's still plenty of life in his wounds, though,
Which he licks open like a dog,
Forgiving but not forgetting.
Born bad like Topsy, he says,
So bent on doing good
Sometimes he can't help just doing.

He says his hands are cold,
But his heart crumbles from its own heat
Like an ember,
Warming him, warming me.

His generation is almost gone, now,
And his voice catches in speaking
Of athletes long since wasted.
At night I hear him talk in his sleep:
Setting a long life to rights,
Lecturing friends and family
(Mostly ghosts)
On how things should have been.
At breakfast, less certain,
He wonders whether he did right in May of '23
                                    — or was it '24?
And laughs at himself,
At the puzzle.

I now call on Bill Bentinck-Smith, my dear friend and adoptive classmate, to elucidate some of that puzzle.   W.H.B.

2

HOFER AND HARVARD

IT IS A TEMPTATION to try to tell Philip Hofer's story in terms of the many apt and entertaining anecdotes with which he delighted his listeners on every occasion. He loved to spin out a story — especially to decorate it with the social history, or the unusual traits, of his chief characters. So we could try to spin out the story of his life.

There is a picture of him at age five. or six on the Camden shore of Penobscot Bay finding sea worms under the rocks and periwinkles in the tidal pools and plopping them into the finger bowls at breakfast time, his earliest collecting venture.

Another picture would show him flaring up with fury and fists at the prep school bullies who were trying to push him into a trashcan, or working his head off for weeks on Soldiers Field lugging water jugs and sheepskin coats, pushing tackling dummies and blocking-sleds, and running, running, running, only to be cut from the freshman football managerial competition just before the Yale game.

A later picture: helping his army mules drag artillery caissons out of the Kentucky mud. Or back at Harvard for graduate work, discovering that to get a "B" in the history of the printed book you had to take George Parker Winship out to lunch, but if you wanted an "A," you took him out to dinner.

Still another picture — through a mix-up in railroad schedules, the young lovers Bunnie Heckscher and Philip Hofer, with their chaperone absent, having to spend a totally chaste night in adjoining rooms in a Lugano hotel, talking to each other by rapping on the wall. And then getting engaged the next day in the St. Gothard tunnel.

Picture Philip, family man, casting caution aside to stand up for principle against the power of the Morgans and Belle da Costa Greene and resigning his assistant directorship at

3

the Morgan Library for an uncertain future. For which Harvard will be eternally grateful.

Picture the glorious confabulation that wickedly hot summer day in 1940 when Arthur Houghton told Hofer, Jackson and Metcalf that he would build the Houghton Library.

Or the tales of travel. They need the full P. Hofer treatment, not a hasty summary. Remember the wonderful anecdote concerning the Japanese umbrellas purchased in 1920 by his father in mist-soaked Nikko after protracted haggling about the price? At his mother's request they were specially decorated by the shopkeeper for each family member with identifying calligraphy. On the street, snickers and pointed fingers followed them. When at last they got back to the hotel, the legends were translated. His father's umbrella said, "Vulgar barbarian who beats down honest Japanese merchant," his mother's, "Fat wife who thinks she has a new idea," and Philip's, "My name is little me too, me too, me too!"

He could keep a listener spellbound with his account of trying to buy a manuscript from the bed-ridden Sir Sydney Cockerell. And perhaps the gem of them all, replete with family lineages and stately homes, is the adventure with the papers of Thomas Frognall Dibden, the English antiquary. This caper, totally spoiled by trying to summarize it, brought William Alexander Jackson and Hofer to the country seat of Earl Spencer, grandfather of Princess Di. By mistake the Harvard representatives got locked in the house, and, not wishing to trouble their grumpy host, had to escape through a second-floor window, down a vine and a waterspout, carrying Jackson's briefcase and looking like a couple of cat burglars. These are the bare facts. The story requires the Hofer touch.

Many similar gems came from his collecting adventures. He designed a whole talk, "The Confessions of a Compulsive Collector," around an amusing anthology of collecting stories. But despite these high points, his files reveal the care and selectivity in his book buying. His prudence with Harvard money. His decisiveness in turning down an offer that did not meet what he deemed a library standard in terms of quality and condition. He almost always made purchases item by item — never bulk lots. He always pleaded for special consideration and an "educational discount" of at least ten percent on booksellers' items. But his colleagues wondered if the dealers did not simply raise the initial price on any Hofer offering.

It took a year of patience and hard bargaining before he was able to obtain in February 1940 at a cost of $2000 the first edition of *Struwwelpeter* with the privilege of selecting thirty-seven other noteworthy illustrated children's books from Walter Schatzki's collection. When the bookseller friend spoke of wanting to be "generous" in the transaction, Hofer snapped back, "It seems foolish to me to talk of 'generosity' in an affair which, it is quite clear, is a business matter. I expect people in business to charge all that they can get, and I find that they generally do. . . . You are asking what you think you can get — against which I have no complaint, except any suggestion that the motive is other than what it is. . . ."

Or in 1944 to Schatzki again, "Do you still have the American calligraphic drawing of a deer and if so, what is your *best* price?" Philip obtained this treasure for $83, and it has long since paid back its asking price by sales of hundreds of Christmas card reproductions at the front desk of Houghton.

Philip's passion for gathering materials that seemed important for the graphic arts, or in some instances just because their shape, color, or tactile quality pleased him, was unceasing. He recognized this irresistible drive. "I have spent personally over two thousand dollars in the last month or so," he told William A. Jackson in 1959. "To my horror I computed yesterday that I gave to the Library this year in money and books over $54,000. It is true madness and I shall have to slow down."

He never did!

A favorite possession was a lovely Holbein watercolor roundel — perhaps originally made by the artist for a decorative box — which Philip commissioned Rudolph Ruzicka to duplicate for his "best book label" — "a miracle of craftsmanship" printed with seven wood blocks marvelously recreating the original in color and delicacy. This drawing shows the struggling figure of Tantalus striving to reach the golden apples and to drink the water which constantly eludes him. Philip adopted it to emphasize "the fate of the born collector who can never satisfy his thirst for acquisition."

Three remarkable people, each in his own way generous beyond praise, were the builders of this library within the Harvard library — Houghton, its founder; Jackson, its first Librarian and "grand acquisitor"; and Hofer, who created within it a study center for the graphic arts modeled after that in the British Museum, then unique in the United States and now, after fifty years, one of the great resources of its kind in the world. Indeed it would not be immoderate to argue, without diminishing the achievement of others, that Philip Hofer has earned a place in the history of the Harvard College Library unmatched by any in its 350 years of existence. Certainly as meticulous scholar, generous donor, shrewd bookman, and insatiable connoisseur-collector, there is no one of his spirit and quality in all of Harvard's history.

Library books and manuscripts by the thousands, book plates, book funds and endowments will continue to bear Philip's name and that of his life's companion, Frances L. Hofer. Fogg Museum drawings, prints, scrolls and other objects are further testimony to their generosity.

Yet merely to state that Philip Hofer was an insatiable collector, a munificent donor, a compassionate teacher, and a loyal colleague fails to do full justice to a remarkable personality. There have been few Harvard people more undeviatingly loyal to their alma mater. He was Harvard crimson double-dyed. Over and over again when he reflected on his long and intellectually exciting career, he pictured his real life starting when he arrived in Cambridge from Cincinnati as a freshman in 1917. He came alive at Harvard and made many friends, even achieved pinnacles of undergraduate recognition. He was for a year vice-president of his class. He was chosen president of Phillips Brooks House; he was named varsity hockey manager, member of the Student Council, and editor of the *Harvard Register*. More important to his future and Harvard's, he discovered the joy of possessing books of consequence, particularly illustrated books. And all this despite the fact that the United States entry into World War I sent him for a time into army service.

After graduation, parental pressure pushed him into a not too successful year at Harvard Business School and then five years in the coal business in Cleveland. But even this was a useful prelude, for he made some wonderfully stimulating friends, he increased his contacts and purchases in the book world, and he became a shrewd investor. Prompted by a promising tip and helped by a small loan from his mother, he gambled boldly in the pre-depression stock market and in a surprisingly short time made himself financially independent and nearly as rich as his father. His parents, then, had no reason to stand in the way of his ambition for an academic career. After a year and a half as a Harvard graduate student in fine arts, there followed marriage — the beginning of a happy union of forty-seven years — the birth of a splendid son, four years as head of the Spencer Collection at the New York Public Library, and three and a half years as assistant director of the Morgan. Now a collector of importance and an established scholar in his field, he was ready for the next step. In 1938, at age forty, he was invited to join William A. Jackson at Harvard under the new Director of the University Library, Keyes DeWitt Metcalf, Hofer's former associate at the New York Public.

Metcalf's objective was to find imaginative solutions for Harvard's library space. Jackson's mission was to bring order and purpose into the acquisition, care and administration of scarce materials, and Hofer's to renew the Friends of the Library, assist Jackson in every possible way, and with a free hand to develop a department of printing and graphic arts along the lines Hofer had long conceived. This was a partnership of common cause and common interest which lasted until Jackson's death in 1964 — a wonderfully complementary working friendship. With an ever widening correspondence, Hofer became a skillful publicist, a shrewd trader in the book markets, a patron of book artists and typographers, a discriminating scholar, a bibliographer, essayist and critic, an editor and publisher, a teacher and encourager of youth. Jackson leaned heavily on this energetic and reliable colleague whose tastes and impulses so helpfully supplemented his own, and whose insatiable appetite for books and generous intentions toward his alma mater were arguably unique in his field. In addition to his Houghton curatorship, he served for two decades as lecturer on Fine Arts and for fourteen years as Secretary of the Fogg Museum. Long an associate of Adams House, he was for one term its acting Master. Although his formal Harvard career ended on June 30, 1968, he continued to occupy his famous subterranean lair in Houghton until his death in 1984.

For more than two decades Philip Hofer literally gave his services to Harvard in return for almost complete freedom to accomplish his ambitions for the Library. This status did not appreciably change when the Corporation, at Paul Buck's insistence, made him a salaried offer in the mid-1950s. His not entirely uncomplaining generosity as a modestly ranked volunteer presented to him definite advantages over the library authorities, since he could expect appropriate departmental administrative assistance and was able to come and go as he wished, travel widely on Harvard business, and pursue cultural and philanthropic work outside the University. These latter activities provided a necessary outlet for his natural concern for other people and contrasted with the intense self-absorption of his daily work with the library.

He collected friends and acquaintances of a vast variety and consumed many hours conversing or corresponding with them. His outgoing mail was particularly awesome, for in addition to a heavy official correspondence (dictated), most of his personal letter-writing was conducted in his clear, neat, bold hand. He particularly valued people in whom he found the basis of common social background, intellectuality, or unusual traits of character and skill. His Heckscher in-laws and their connections made more of a family life for him than he ever found with his parents. There were his colleagues of course — his long close friendship with "the three Bills," Jackson, Cottrell, and Bond. There were scores of booksellers whom he greatly admired and sometimes fought with, and his loyalties to his Harvard classmates. A year or so before his death he donated a beech tree for the Harvard Yard in tribute to his friend, Hermon Dunlap Smith, and his classmates of '21.

For many years he was a freshman adviser, a volunteer job which in some cases meant only checking study cards, but in Hofer's conscientious way produced carefully composed character sketches for the Dean of Freshmen, and conscientious concern blended with common sense advice for those who truly sought his help. Typical is the following quick memorandum from Philip Hofer on one of his advisees forty years ago: "He cares for the arts in the same way that I do and is fully aware of his ability in that line . . . I stressed steady work, no cutting and plenty of exercise. . . ."

For many years he shared with Jackson and Bond teaching stints in The History of the Printed Book, a departmental course in English and Fine Arts requiring rather close contact with the students. Less formally he was generous with his time and help to a steady stream of individual students, some of whom became protégés and a few, like Isaiah Jackson, the symphonic conductor, became Bunnie's and Philip's so-called "adopted" children.

Beyond the collector-teacher's first-hand efforts to spread knowledge of the history of printed and illustrated books,

Philip was often studying, lecturing and writing. He once remarked that he had a hand in about fifty publications as author or publisher. The number is actually almost three times that, according to official count. These show great variety: of course there are his works of permanent importance, such as the books on Edward Lear and Baroque book illustration. Others bear touches of his guiding hand, such as the Museum of Fine Arts exhibition and catalogue on the book artists of the period 1860 to 1960 prepared by Eleanor Garvey. His influence is evident also in Ruth Mortimer's splendid catalogues of Hofer's sixteenth-century French and Italian books and Anne Anninger's check list of Hofer's Spanish books, issued after his death. We should also mention the scores of professional articles, reviews and critical introductions, as well as the memoirs and intimate essays which he wrote in his pensive hours and shared with friends. An important example of this reflective writing is a five-page leaflet "On the Nature of Love" intended "to clarify my own thinking and to eradicate my inhibitions . . . as a gift for understanding friends, and for such young of our land as I can reach."

Along with Philip's natural sympathy for other people, and a native strain of sociability, went the gift of conversation. Having used all his senses as a traveler and observer, and blest with a retentive memory, he brought wit, liveliness, and informed opinion to his social intercourse. Of a dinner party he remarked, "Conversation sparkled. . . . we dashed in and out of concepts, stories which were to the point, and various summer plans. . . ." Conversation always dashed and sparkled when Hofer was around, although sometimes he reprimanded himself for talking so much and resolved to be a better listener.

Toward the end of his life Philip estimated that his personal and departmental library, carefully and persistently selected and refined over a period of more than fifty years, totaled almost 25,000 volumes. The bulk of these, including his valuable research library, were given to Harvard in his lifetime, the balance by bequest. One of the glories of the collection are the manuscripts, almost a thousand in number when single leaves are counted.

It is impossible to speculate with any degree of accuracy on the monetary value of the Hofer collection. Although the patron himself did not consider most of the items bargains when he bought them, he recognized that the manuscripts, of course, and many of the books would never again be on the market, and as the years passed his extraordinary perceptiveness about importance and scarcity eventually made his collection priceless. His life's work is indeed a triumphant success, for, when he began, the Harvard Library had few illustrated books, very few medieval illuminated manuscripts and little Oriental material. Today it is probably the principle collection in this country for illustrated books of the sixteenth, seventeenth and nineteenth centuries and is increasing its strength in the eighteenth and twentieth centuries. It comprises all areas of pictorial interest and includes writing books, typefounders' specimen books, printers' manuals, and to some extent book papers, papermaking and binding materials.

Yes, our friend Philip Hofer remains a living presence among us, and his name will endure at Harvard as long as his university continues to honor books and learning. As long as scholars of the present and future seek here ways to consult and study his collection and employ what they find to illuminate their own work and to add to the scope of knowledge. As long as students and connoisseurs come to this place in a spirit of curiosity, joy, wonder, and gratitude.

At one of the Fogg Museum's swellest parties in his honor in 1984, Philip responded to the collective laudation by throwing a linen napkin over his head and face in mock modesty. In truth, however, he really loved to be loved. So we say, with love: Well done, Philip Hofer! Well done, and many, many thanks!   W. B-S.

N O COLLECTOR *who amounts to anything, and no library that has claims to greatness, can possibly succeed without the close friendship and knowledgeable help of skillful and learned booksellers, who are all too often regarded as mere background, spearcarriers for those whose bibliophilic exploits take center stage. What a misjudgment! And one that I have another quotation to offset, from the long poem,* Jubilate Agno, *by another old acquaintance of mine, Christopher Smart:*

> For I bless God in the libraries of the learned and for all the booksellers in the world.

The collector or librarian who has not been educated by booksellers can scarcely be said to have been educated at all. No one knew this better or echoed Smart's sentiments more devoutly than Philip Hofer; and to deal with this aspect of his career, I call upon another old friend of his and mine, Lucien Goldschmidt, now retired but still the dean of the sellers of prints and illustrated books in New York City.   W.H.B.

MEMORIES OF A COMPULSIVE COLLECTOR

I T IS A GREAT HONOR to be standing here in this setting
and to recall for a few moments the figure of Philip
Hofer. I assume that most of those present have known him,
and some have undoubtedly had lasting ties of common interest and personal affection. What I can say for my relations
with him is twofold. In the first place, I can look back with
great pleasure and satisfaction on a contact that lasted for
over forty years. We had apparently what the French call *des
atomes crochus*, interlocking atoms. On the other hand, there
was a process of learning going on. I learned a great deal
from him, and, occasionally, because I was able to display to
him some object that he had not seen before, I was given
the chance to extend his range of interest.

I have been involved in buying and selling books, prints,
and drawings over a period of more than fifty years,
through a succession of upheavals, developments from
depression to prosperity, in France and the United States.
The personalities encountered exert a fascination just as the
objects do. You wish to understand them, to find the key
to the motivation that is behind their purchases, in order to
assist the collectors to the best of your ability. Striking figures stand out in my mind. I can recall great bibliophiles
like Louis Barthou, in his last year as foreign minister of
France, who was the victim of political murder; the Swiss,
Martin Bodmer, one-time president of the International Red
Cross; and, closer to home, Lessing J. Rosenwald, who so
enriched the National Gallery and the Library of Congress;
and Robert Woods Bliss and Mildred Bliss, who made the
Dumbarton Oaks museum and its landscaped setting. But
even against such personalities, to mention Philip Hofer
means to see a separate entity, a person quite unlike the
others. The convergence of the immense eagerness to know,

to learn, to observe with enjoyment, with the desire to create an edifice that would help others to take the steps that he himself had taken; that is most uncommon.

There was always that wish to appreciate and to teach others to appreciate as well, and this disposition I believe is exemplary. Those who have assembled a collection over a period of many years are often rather set in their ways, and they are reluctant to widen the scope of their interests. Philip, however, constantly redefined the outlines of his field. He remained willing to examine what was new to him, no matter how obscure it might be. It meant also that he was ready to discard what he saw in a different light when he was confronted with new acquisitions or newly-established correlations, or when he found a more perfect example or an object of greater educational value.

Whatever the changes were, he strove for synthesis, not disjunction. He could recommend the sculptured Buddhas of Bamian in Afghanistan as readily as he stressed the beauty of the Tuppo Aesop, which is in the present show. Or the photographs of Baldus in the series of views of the Northern French railroad line. He gave me details about the monasteries to be visited in Macedonia around Lake Ochrid-Monastir, pressing me to see their singular merits. Such a wide range of interests was an attribute of his complex, many-layered personality. It could be said that, like a scenic design, he might reveal different backdrops in various colors and of graded intensity. You suspected, however, that the ultimate element of the scenery would not be revealed. In his make-up, justified pride and self-assurance, the readiness to judge without delay merged with his sense for subtle distinction. His feeling of love and awe for the great creations of mankind and his fascination with the multitude of human endeavors were truly unusual. His personality ran counter to the stereotyped psychology of characters as they appear in films, or television, or the comics. There was no one quite like him. It was our good fortune that we could enjoy his company over so many years. If he felt you were willing to meet him on this ground, ready to give the best of your knowledge and what understanding you might have achieved, he was very appreciative and responded with a mixture of candor and enthusiasm. You could count on sharing pleasure when you came together with him, looking at objects of essential harmony and recognizing them for their merit. In front of a shelf of books, what keenness of vision! The hawks circling overhead dive suddenly to seize the objects of their desire. His means of selecting were equally darting and forceful, and this comparison is meant with respect and a lasting admiration. In a similar manner, when he showed some of his recent finds in his grotto at the Houghton Library, how clearly he saw their appeal and perhaps also their flaws. To be sure, there were other moods as well. He could be nostalgic; he could feel melancholy, loss, or disillusion. At Christmastime once, we sent him a copy of Seymour Haden's book, *About Etching*, with season's greetings. He wrote a touching letter, recollecting how his mother had bought a china paper impression of Shere Mill Pond way back in 1910 that hung in his parents' library in Cincinnati, and that he was happy he still owned it in 1969. He went on to say, "Memories, memories. . . *à la recherche du temps perdu*," adding, "*pour jamais*." He liked to exercise his French, and at an opening of a French drawing show at the National Gallery, he came over to my wife and for a good while conversed with her in French, just to enjoy the fact that he could still do it with fluency and without rustiness.

He was not just generous to Harvard, but also to his friends. Once when I had done an appraisal for the Houghton Library that pleased him very much, he sent me a handsome Japanese eighteenth-century manuscript illustrated with the painted images of two poets sitting on the seashore.

The collector, the amateur, and the critic must have access to that region that I would like to call the palace of imagination. Out of the thousands of objects they see, only a limited number can call out to them. What may seem a romantic flourish when so described does indeed take place: a pang of anticipation, an agitation linked to the recognition that here is one of those ardently desired books, manuscripts, prints, foretold in the palace of imagination. The discovery sets off a response that can be anticipated only in a general way, with a dim apprehension. It was not inscribed in any list of masterpieces established by others, no matter how expert. Great scholars and great collectors must keep open this accessibility. It allows creations of vast diversity to arouse them. In this case, it could be a twelfth-century Byzantine manuscript, or an early undescribed state of Piranesi. It might be an intricate record of a Baroque festivity with unfolding plates, a recent *livre de peintre*, a French or Italian Renaissance book, an Eastern jug. It didn't matter. If it had merit, he saw it. And what you see in this exhibition testifies to his creative vision, the vastness of his aim and his devotion to form. It is not easy to be able to leave 20,000 valuable items (by valuable, I do not mean commercial value, but value because of intrinsic merit), as he has done. And, as you know, when William Jackson wrote an essay for *The Book Collector* twenty-four years before Philip's death, he had already by that time given 10,000 items to Harvard.

There were many areas, some which had been recognized before, but others, like the drawings for book illustration, that were then really neglected. When people saw them, they said, "Well, it is sort of a beginning, but it's not the real thing. Let's just buy the book, or the finished print." But Philip saw that no matter what, the engraving, the etching, the woodcut, or the lithograph, however skillful or lively, was the result of a process used either by the artist himself or by the professional hired for rendering the work. This procedure dries out the upsurge of the first vision. The melting quality of the drawing generally diminishes when transferred to the copperplate, the woodblock, or the stone. Philip Hofer and his wife Frances made a significant contribution in forming their collection of drawings for book illustration and giving it to the Houghton Library. A handsome catalogue by David P. Becker was produced for that occasion. In our century, the use of professional graphic translators sharply decreased, as the images were more and more created by the artists themselves in the way in which they saw them. Still more recently, I am sorry to say, these illustrations are often the result of sleight of hand, even of manners and techniques hostile to the work that is unique and done by the artist.

In a life devoted to acquisition, a concern for the economic impact of one's purchases cannot be avoided. There must be a framework within which judgments on prices correlate with the piece selected. While Philip could have said with Wallace Stevens that "Materialism is an old story and an indifferent one," because the overriding importance was the recognition of beauty and intellectual stimulation, it is true that he was determined to strike a good bargain. He wanted to keep his project afloat without compromising the sources of revenue, and he achieved that aim well.

One of the most outstanding areas that he was influential in rescuing from neglect (others have been mentioned) was the Baroque period of book illustration, unpopular until then, rejected by both the conservatives, who wanted either the sixteenth-century or the eighteenth-century productions, and by the modernists, who aimed at Bauhaus-like purity. Philip Hofer gave Baroque books a place of distinction. These often large and unwieldy books, which began in the last years of the sixteenth century and did not vanish until the early eighteenth century, were often treated with just a few derogatory words. It is hard to believe some of the things you can read in older reference books, speeding over the seventeenth century in three sentences. In the past thirty-seven years since the appearance of Philip's book, the compositions of Rubens and Poussin, Callot and Bosse, Caron and Jaspar Isaac, Romeyn de Hooghe, Rembrandt and De Passe, Tempesta and Coriolano, to name just a few, have been recognized the way he recognized them, for their boldness and their strength. This subject had a powerful appeal for me, and I was happy to issue a catalogue of such books very shortly after Philip's book appeared in 1951.

A wonderful sense of discovery led him shortly after the Second World War to spot, in a sale at the now defunct Hodgson auction house in London, a volume of illuminated emblems by Jacques Bailly, a court painter of Louis XIV. The Louvre had the work that was actually completed for the king. It was proudly displayed on many occasions. But what Hodgson sold — and positively for a pittance — appears to have been a second set, probably made for Colbert in 1663-1665, with fewer leaves than were done for the king, but just as beautiful in execution. These wonderful milky white sheets of vellum, with their handsome calligraphy and the pristine colors of Bailly, are an outstanding achievement. They made hardly a stir at Hodgson's, but the knowledge of the Louvre manuscript allowed Philip to decide that they had to be its younger brothers.

About the exhibition that brought the modern *livre de peintre* to the attention of the American public, you have already heard a few words, and its extraordinary catalogue is a standard book now. *The Artist and the Book* was the first great exhibition of the modern illustrated book. When it was shown in 1961, none of those involved could have known the long lasting influence it would exert.

In the coat of arms of the Dutch Royal House of Orange-Nassau appear the words, "Je maintiendrai." Philip Hofer promised to himself to maintain, to keep secure the works he valued. Well beyond that, he gave to the objects he acquired a status that made them desirable, when they had not been regarded that way before. Others were able to study what had fascinated him. This continued interest in the best typographical productions of the past centuries was most foresighted, now that the great tradition of typographic composition has fallen a victim to the chilling rule of photo-composition. Philip's taste for the work of printing and illustration of the sixteenth century led him to strengthen in every way the Harvard holdings, particularly in French and Italian illustrated books, and there was a mention before of Ruth Mortimer's wonderful catalogues. Eleanor Garvey is currently working on a third catalogue, of the Italian eighteenth century, still a very little-known field, which so far has only been treated very generally by Morazzoni. Philip was very innovative and farsighted, because Italian eighteenth-century illustration has all the grace and all the fantasy of the better-known French works.

A great amount of building occurred in Western Europe in the eighteenth century. Rulers meant to signal their might and wealth the way large corporations now plan stunning headquarters. What was relatively rare, however, were proposals to redevelop a section of an older city to make it more serviceable and up-to-date. At one time we were issuing a description of architectural drawings from our stock. Philip Hofer immediately noticed a drawn urban renewal plan for Bordeaux of about 1793, and went ahead of the specialists to obtain it at a time when such works had not attained their present noble status (we are speaking of 1965). Even early photography, then a subject never broached, never discussed, was discovered by him. I do not believe there were twenty collectors of photography in the entire world in 1935. In that year, however, Philip Hofer met a dealer in London who showed him these things, and with that intuitive grasp, he immediately bought, within a few weeks, what I think was a distinguished collection of early nineteenth-century French and English photography. He did not collect photography later on, but it was always in his mind, and I remember one day when the Morgan Library did that beautiful show called "French Primitive Photography," he took the catalogue in his hands and said, "Lucien, you see, this is what Andrew Wyeth would have liked to do, only he can't."

His stories, as has been pointed out, are wonderful. There is one that I greatly enjoyed. At one point, the Duke of Holstein had offered Harvard, not as a gift, nor as a potential purchase, but with the intention of renting out, what he said were outstanding materials of the American Revolution. Philip Hofer, together with a distinguished German bookseller, Helmuth Domizlaff, decided to go and take a look. They went to the Duke, who lived in great splendor with liveried footmen and all that, and when they were shown his "treasures," one glance convinced them both that they were not real; they were spurious. The disappointment was keen and the utmost polite firmness was necessary to leave the scene of disenchantment without disturbing the host. Domizlaff then, as a means of reviving Philip's spirits, proposed to drive to Schweinfurt to give him the opportunity of making the acquaintance of the foremost book collector and print collector in West Germany, Otto Schaefer. Thus this clouded journey ended very pleasantly for all. Philip told this story with great gusto and thought he learned from it various salutary lessons. In such retelling of his experiences, the conciseness of his style and his wit showed to best advantage. It is also these qualities and their development in the pursuit of art that are mirrored in his clear and forceful handwriting. Their reflection in the handsome shaping of the letters and Philip's epistolary skill remained undiminished throughout the years.

Shortly before his death in November 1984, he wrote, "I still care a great deal for those many who have helped me, and for the few I have been, perhaps, able to help during my long life." In this sentence we can feel his willingness and his need to attract and be attracted by the bright and active of all groups. His looking at art, his reading of books, and his fervent fascination by places near and far, filled with people, all these inclinations were coherent and formed a recognizable pattern. Not for him the ivory tower. He felt, I should say, what the Portuguese poet, Fernando Pessoa wrote in his *Maritime Ode*, "All faces are singular, and nothing so communicates the sense of the sacred as to look at people a great deal."   L.G.

I HAVE NEVER KNOWN *anyone with a more pronounced sense of fun and mischief than Philip Hofer, but it was underlaid by a strain of melancholy that surfaced from time to time. This combination inspired the direction of his collecting in more than one way, but before we explore that, it may not be inappropriate to quote from Robert Burton's* Anatomy of Melancholy,

Part 2, section 2, member 4, which treats of books and libraries as part of the cure of melancholy:

. . . So sweet is the delight of study, the more learning [men] have, (as he that hath a dropsie, the more he drinks, the thirstier he is) the more they covet to learn; . . . the longer they live, the more they are enamoured of the Muses. Heinsius, the keeper of the library at Leiden in Holland, was mewed up in it all the year long; and that which to thy thinking should have bred a loathing, caused in him a greater liking. "I no sooner" (saith he) "come into the library, but I bolt the door to me, excluding lust, ambition, avarice, and all such vices, whose nurse is Idlenesse the mother of Ignorance, and Melancholy her self; and in the very lap of eternity, amongst so many divine souls, I take my seat, with so lofty a spirit and sweet content, that I pitty all our great ones . . . that know not this happinesse." I am not ignorant in the mean time (notwithstanding this which I have said) how barbarously and basely for the most part our ruder gentry esteem of libraries and books, how they neglect and contemn so great a treasure, so inestimable a benefit, as Aesop's cock did the jewel he found in the dunghil, and all through error, ignorance, and want of education. [v.I, p.424]

One thinks of Philip's fierce defenses of his vocation and avocation, and of how he retreated, like Heinsius, into his fabulous cave two floors directly below us in the Houghton stacks, to recruit his spirits and to protect himself from a cruder world. One thinks also of the parallels between him and Edward Lear, an artist and writer for whom he felt a particular affinity and a profound admiration. Affinity? It was almost identification, as one sees in the dedication *of his* Edward Lear as a Landscape Draughtsman *published in 1967: "To F. L.H., without whom I might have been as lonely as Edward Lear."*

Charles Ryskamp, long a friend of Philip's, one-time Professor of English at Princeton University, later brilliant director of the Pierpont Morgan Library (where, two directors earlier, Philip had been a staff member in his pre-Harvard University days), is now Director of The Frick Collection in New York. He will speak to us about Hofer and Lear. W.H.B.

HOW PLEASANT TO KNOW MR. HOFER

W HEN I LOOK back on the years I knew Philip Hofer, I see that there was a network of ties connecting us. There was his schoolboy friend Wendell Davis, whom I knew well in Princeton; he had roomed with Philip for six years at Pomfret, and through all of their time at Harvard. There were much younger friends of his, passionate acquisitors, who formed remarkable collections of books and silver and porcelain, like Bob Pirie, or Pre-Columbian art, like Gillett Griffin. There was Priscilla Barker, my assistant for more than ten years at the Morgan Library, who came to New York from the Department of Printing and Graphic Arts, where she had worked closely with Philip Hofer and with Elli Garvey. There was the Morgan Library itself — where he had had four brilliant, stormy years as the Assistant Director to the legendary Belle Green. One of the things which made me happiest during my nearly eighteen years as Director of the Morgan Library was bringing Philip Hofer back into that fold, and, I hope, mostly healing the wounds made fifty years earlier.

I find it impossible not to talk about myself, and my friends, when discussing either Philip Hofer or Edward Lear. Books make the best friends. To that most of us present would agree. And books also make the best friendships. Those in my own life who most intimately drew around them the net of friendship were Geoffrey Keynes, Donald Hyde, and Philip Hofer. Each was an utterly devoted bookman, and among the finest collectors of his time; and each of them depended on friendship and built friendships in a way incomparable to any others I have known, except to each other.

It was Edward Lear who first led me to Philip Hofer. It is therefore, I believe, most appropriate that I speak about

Lear today, and not of any other of Philip's many interests, or friends, or his incredible variety of acquisitions. Surely one of the most valuable keys to knowing Philip Hofer — the man and the collector — and to celebrating this man, is in his collecting and writing about Edward Lear. The diversity of Philip Hofer's moods and passions — the industrious, buoyant, effervescent personality which co-existed with the sensitive and lonely — are mirrored in his relationship with the works and life of Edward Lear. Philip himself often said that he grew up painfully shy and alone, and he keenly identified with the shyness and loneliness of Lear. Of both it may be said that they were especially marked by profound kindness and by a wonderful capacity for making friends. They also had a phenomenal ability, in quite different ways, for linking pictures and text, the graphic line and the word.

I cannot tell you when Philip Hofer first began to read and study the works of Edward Lear. We know that the first " 'rare' and *illustrated* book" that he ever purchased was in the early autumn of 1917, as a freshman at Harvard. But it was not until 1929 that he — or anyone else — had a true opportunity to buy drawings by Lear. The dispersal of the Lear drawings known to us today stems almost wholly from two important sales in that year. The first was held in February and March, by order of the daughters of Sir Franklin Lushington, a lifelong friend of Lear; it was a sale which included a large number of books, manuscripts, prints, drawings, and thirty volumes of his personal diary. Three months later, Philip Hofer bought in a London bookshop a scrapbook from this sale; it had "over fifty landscape drawings, dozens of nonsense sketches, and seven manuscript poems." He bought this, as he wrote, "for the absurdly low figure of sixty pounds! No demand from the British collecting world had yet developed. The bookseller's shelves, in fact, were glutted — and this in a year of high prosperity throughout the English-speaking world, when some English nineteenth-century 'first editions' reached an all-time high in market value."

The second important group of Lear's works came up for sale eight months later, in November, when a much larger collection of his drawings, that owned by the Earl of Northbrook, was auctioned at Sotheby's. (It was the Earl who, as Viceroy of India, had invited Lear to come there to visit and to draw.) During 1929, and in the early 1930s, three men in particular took advantage of these sales and created very important collections: the first was Johannes Gennadius, who concentrated on Greek drawings, of which there are now over 250 in Athens from his collection. And then there were two men from New York: William B. Osgood Field, who was encouraged to collect Lear by Philip Hofer; and finally Hofer himself. The collections of Field and Hofer were brought together at Harvard in the Department of Printing and Graphic Arts through simultaneous gifts at the opening of the Houghton Library in 1942. The greater part of the Harvard collection came from the Northbrook provenance; it now numbers over 3500 drawings as well as thirty volumes of diaries, from 1858 to 1887, two volumes of journals in India and one volume of a journal in Crete. The collection at Harvard is surely the finest in the world, and there seems no chance of any other place forming one of comparable variety, depth, and number.

It is hard for me to talk of my own handful of drawings by Lear in this connection, but it is necessary for me to do so to explain how I came to know Philip Hofer. In the mid-1950s (I cannot now recall the exact year), I bought two very large pen and wash drawings by Edward Lear, views of the bay of Naples, from the sea and from land. I had bought engravings and etchings on rare occasions since I was a boy of thirteen, but these were my first drawings. Their purchase resulted in my strong interest in English drawings, which I pursued as avidly as possible during the next two decades, preferring often to buy English drawings even to buying English books or manuscripts. My purchase of two drawings by Lear was therefore a turning point in my life, just as the Lear scrapbook was for Philip Hofer in 1929.

I was proud of my drawings, and at the earliest opportunity I went to see Donald Gallup, whom I already knew, the eminent bibliographer and curator of American literature, who had in his apartment at Yale a very large collection of drawings by Lear. About the same time, I went to call on Philip Hofer in the Department of Printing and Graphic Arts, and I began to study the vast collection at Harvard. Hofer and I had lunch together; we went to Boston bookstores on Beacon Hill and to the antique shops along Charles Street; and I spent — gladly — much more than I should have. A friendship began, and my interest and knowledge of the illustrated book, of manuscripts and drawings, grew enormously. This visit was no doubt crucial in my life.

I am convinced that I owe significant changes in my career more to the development of friendships like that with Philip Hofer, than I do to my formal education, or my teaching or writings. My life at Princeton, at the Morgan Library, and now at The Frick Collection, has evolved in most important ways from the shared experiences of books and art that I have had with friends like Philip Hofer, Geoffrey Keynes, Wilmarth Lewis, and Donald Hyde. I am therefore pleased today to be asked to pay tribute to Philip Hofer, and to be able also to speak of these other outstanding bookmen.

I will *not* now try to say what Edward Lear has meant, or means, to me; but I should like to try to indicate something of Philip Hofer's exceptional appreciation and understanding of the works of this artist and writer. Philip's interest resulted in his publication of fifteen articles, essays, booklets, and books about Lear; these first appeared in 1935 and went on until 1977. His passion for Lear also played a major role in building Harvard's great collection. The sales in 1929 provided incredible opportunities for collecting, which Philip Hofer immediately seized upon. When he saw an unusual opportunity for acquisitions — for himself or for Harvard — he could act — and did act — with remarkable decisiveness, and he also could move into new areas of collecting with absolute assurance about quality and importance. He knew, almost by instinct, what was valuable, but was unappreciated; and, it must be said, what was a bargain. All this is true of his reaction to the sales of 1929, and his determination to build his Lear collection and that at Harvard. His quick and sure decision and his adventurous spirit in learning about new artists, unknown books, and little recognized areas of collecting were characteristic of his life as a collector and of his development of this Department.

Coupled with this acquisitiveness and ability for decision were a knowledge and a love of what he collected which have rarely, if ever, been equalled among the bookmen I have known. This is especially well illustrated in his sympathy and understanding for Lear. When he spoke of Lear, or wrote about him, Philip Hofer seemed to become Lear — to be inside the man himself.

Among the very many things that Lear was, that he was fundamentally a writer as well as a draughtsman was a great source of Lear's strong appeal. One must not forget that Philip Hofer's field of concentration as an undergraduate at Harvard was English literature, and throughout his life he was an avid reader and was deeply appreciative of literary merit. He relished Lear's letters, and delighted in his nonsense verse. He believed that Lear's pre-eminence in originality was in his nonsense writings. He savored the poem about the Yonghy-Bonghy-Bò, and wrote a fine piece about its poetry while his friend Randall Thompson wrote about the music for those verses. I am sure that many of you here can remember how Philip would recite those lines:

On the Coast of Coromandel
Where the early pumpkins blow,
In the middle of the woods

27

Lived the Yonghy-Bonghy-Bò.
Two old chairs, and half a candle, —
One old jug without a handle, —
These were all his worldly goods . . .

Philip cherished Lear's limericks, his nonsense alphabets,
and other poems, like "The Owl and the Pussy-cat," which
I need not repeat to you; nor need I give more than a hint of
such lines as

"How pleasant to know Mr. Lear!"
Who has written such volumes of stuff!
Some think him ill-tempered and queer,
But a few think him pleasant enough.

Among the over two hundred items in the Lear collection donated by Hofer himself, three-fourths were manuscripts of nonsense poetry and prose. How proud Philip
Hofer was that he and Mr. Field, and therefore Harvard,
had gathered together so many of Lear's manuscripts of
these verses, his letters, and his journals.

In many ways, the most impressive publication of Philip
Hofer was his masterly book on *Edward Lear as a Landscape
Draughtsman*, published by Harvard in 1967 and a year later
by Oxford University Press. This work was the first, and
has remained for over two decades the only, study of Lear's
painting and drawing. In it Philip Hofer shows his remarkable ability to put Lear as a landscape draughtsman into that
great British tradition. He understands the whole history of
British traveling artists: from John White, who joined Sir
Walter Raleigh on his second expedition to America in
1585, through the many artists — professional and amateur
— who went on a Grand Tour to Italy during the eighteenth century, to the host of English draughtsmen who
covered Europe, the near East, India, and China in the nineteenth century. Philip Hofer could evaluate not only the
painters and sketchers like Lear, but the travelers who were

chiefly archaeologists or architects. He showed how Lear fitted in with all of these artists, even with figures so obscure that few experts on British art would know them.

For Philip Hofer, "the nearer the time of the first sketch, the stronger and surer the result" in Lear's drawings. Hofer preferred what he called the "sparing, sober, and subtle" pen work or slight touches of color in the first sketches. And he is right that these are usually Lear's most original works of art. His studies of single trees, above all, or those of trees massed on hillsides, reveal "the inner grace," as Hofer wrote, the very nature of each kind of tree. The sketches are not over-elaborated; Lear maintains a skillful balance of the individual parts of the landscape with the total view. And he has an unusual ability to emphasize essential detail. Philip Hofer writes about all of these things with splendid sureness and elegance, and in a most personal style. He dares to make some startling comparisons, and these are very effective. He finds that Lear is like William Blake in that he was "possessed of an inner determination to go his own way." And he was like Rembrandt in that in his drawings he could express himself "in the simplest terms."

In his study of Lear as a landscape draughtsman, Philip Hofer explains succinctly and perceptively the evolution of Lear's topographical style, and in spite of his preference — his love — for Lear, he recognizes the weaknesses of the artist. Perhaps, however, he is too critical of Lear as a painter. He feels that Lear's paintings almost always fail in comparison with his drawings and watercolors. Hofer often speaks of the lifelessness of Lear's canvases and writes that "stiffness . . . characterized nearly all of his large paintings." Unlike the other great American collector of Lear in the past forty years, Donald Gallup, Philip Hofer really did not appreciate these very large landscapes. In 1967 Hofer could write, almost happily, that there was no market for them, while the sketches for which he had paid a few shillings apiece in the early thirties were now worth hundreds — even thousands — of pounds. But there has been a revision in our thinking in recent years, and most of Lear's large canvases are now worth tens of thousands of pounds.

Many recognize that some of the huge works — these awesome vistas of distant mountains, giant gorges, valleys banked with dark trees — have a powerful grandeur. They reveal an assurance in handling a vast scale of landscape that establishes in the viewer a sense of the sublime. The best of Lear's sweeping landscapes "evoke the contrary feelings of attraction and repulsion," which is true of the sublime as it was traditionally conceived. In such canvases Lear shows himself to be a "Painter of Poetical Topography" — the phrase is Lear's own; he used it to describe himself on several occasions. Therefore his achievement is altogether different from the immediate sketch, the direct observation of nature. Yet in its own way, it is no less distinguished.

There are two or three other points which Philip Hofer repeatedly emphasizes when writing about Lear. One is the variety of his accomplishments. I have already touched on this, but it deserves to be stressed here. Philip Hofer believed that Lear was important in the history of nineteenth-century England "because he had so many different facets to his genius." In Hofer's brilliant short introduction to a catalogue of an exhibition of Lear's works shown at the Worcester Art Museum in 1968, we find this final paragraph:

> Edward Lear was not a great painter, but he was a very fine topographical draughtsman. It is really as a combination of letter writer, sensitive poet, intrepid traveler, ornithological, zoological, and botanical draughtsman, amateur musician, widely appreciated pioneer humorist that he adds up to an extremely important Victorian figure. As a human being he was possibly most interesting of all.

Ultimately it was Lear's humanity with which Philip Hofer identified, and the two aspects of deepest concern to him were Lear's loneliness, which co-existed with his extraordinary capacity for friendship. I began by mentioning these characteristics; in conclusion I wish to read a few other sentences from Philip Hofer's writings which relate to them. Lear's biography, he declared, "is essentially that of a lonely man restlessly searching for repose and an unattainable ideal friendship." The fascinating study of Lear as a landscape draughtsman begins with a dedication to Philip's wife Bunny. It reads: "To F. L.H., without whom I might have been as lonely as Edward Lear." The preface to the book and, in fact, the whole text are remarkable for the numerous citations of collectors of Lear's drawings, dozens of persons from many countries, and for the survey of collecting and collections. Most of the persons Philip Hofer names he calls "my friend," and this book is as much a tribute to collector friends as it is to painting and drawing.

The first chapter was separately printed in a beautiful little booklet published by Oxford University Press in 1962. It concludes:

> Finally, if one has ever been lonely oneself, has ever worried long and fruitlessly, one grows to love this shy, humorous, bumbling man, who tried so little to exploit this world and put so much back into it. Just think, that in spite of his asthma, his epilepsy, his weak eyes, the rheumatism he contracted in damp, wild regions where he often went without adequate clothing or cover; this man without money, wife, or child, traveling ceaselessly, worrying, suffering — *just think*, he managed to invent hundreds of word-forms, to popularize the limerick, to dash off, or carefully to compose, up to thirty-five letters a day, to write, illustrate, publish, and largely sell by mail and by subscription, seven travel books, to illustrate four natural history books completely, and many others in part, to write and illustrate six books of highly original nonsense, to write the music and to sing a number of songs, and painfully to fill in each day sixty

large volumes of diaries! All this he did, remember, in addition to several hundred oil paintings (many of them huge) and over ten thousand fairly elaborate drawings.

Finally, he made literally hundreds of friends, a large proportion of whom remained friends for life.

This, gentle reader is achievement! C.R.

M Y LAST QUOTATION *is from the Rosenbach Lectures in Bibliography delivered by Christopher Morley at the University of Pennsylvania in 1931.*

In the Anglican Prayerbook there is a magnificent passage which, by just transposing the accent, leaps to the eye of the booklover. You find it is written that "The first collect for the day, the second collect for peace, the third collect for the grace to live well." . . . Those who collect for the day may perhaps be collecting to sell again tomorrow. In the case of those who collect for peace, possibly one element in their pacification is the unworthy feeling that they have the best existing copy. I hope we are of those who collect for grace.

Philip Hofer was surely one of those who collected for grace. A central component in that grace was his constant willingness to impart his knowledge and connoisseurship to others, particularly to the young. He was, in fact, a very great teacher in Harvard's long tradition of great teachers, and his teaching extended far beyond the university. Yet, by a typical Harvard paradox, he was never officially a Harvard professor: he was never a member of the Faculty of Arts and Sciences. From some points of view, attending faculty meetings is a dubious privilege, but privilege it is; and to my knowledge the only faculty meeting he ever attended was by invitation to read, as Chairman, the official Faculty Minute on the death of W.A. Jackson — from which meeting he then had to retire before other business was transacted. Yet for many an undergraduate, graduate student, colleague, and friend he was the most unforgettable teacher at Harvard. Our last speaker, who did not attend Harvard College any more than I did, but who learned a great deal from Philip Hofer, as did I, is Arthur Vershbow, Boston man of business, eminent collector in much the same field as Philip's, and trustee of numerous cultural organizations. W.H.B.

PHILIP HOFER IN CONTEXT

I AM GOING TO SPEAK to you today about Philip's collecting, but before I do, I'd like to emphasize how much fun it was to be with Philip.

I remember going to his office one day late in the afternoon. He was sitting at his desk, looking gloomily at his large old-fashioned three-to-a-page checkbook. He looked up to me and said, "Arthur, I'm *desperately* poor."

And another story: Philip, Elli Garvey, David Becker, Charlotte and I, some years ago, were all together at the opening and dedication of the new East Wing of the National Gallery in Washington. President Jimmy Carter had just dedicated the building, and we were all in the receiving line to be greeted by the President's wife, Rosalynn Carter. As we went down the line, a Marine Guard would ask us our names and introduce each guest to Mrs. Carter. Philip was just ahead of us, and when he was introduced to Mrs. Carter he said, "Oh Mrs. Carter, I had such a lovely evening with you just a few weeks ago at your charming little apartment at the Watergate." Well, she looked rather puzzled, but was very polite and said, "It's so nice to meet you." After we had gone through the line, Charlotte asked, "Philip, what was that you were saying about 'a little apartment in the Watergate?' She lives in the *White House!*" "Oh!" he said, "I thought the lady was Mrs. Carter Brown (wife of the Director of the National Gallery)." Charlotte said, "No, that was *Mrs. Jimmy Carter*, wife of the President of the United States!" "I must apologize right away," he said, and rushed off to talk to *Mrs. Carter Brown*. Later we asked him why he was apologizing to Mrs. Carter Brown. He replied, "I apologized because I took her for an older woman."

About the year 1630, the year of the founding of Boston and Cambridge, the Scottish poet William Drummond of Hawthornden wrote a paper entitled *Of Libraries*, containing this statement: "Libraries are as forests, in which not only tall Cedars and Oaks are to be found, but Bushes too, and dwarfish Shrubs."

Philip Hofer, in his collecting, sought and acquired both tall Cedars and Oaks, *and* Bushes and dwarfish Shrubs. He justly admired the Cedars and Oaks: the great books sought out by generations of collectors are truly great, and we see many of them here at Houghton in the cases, and described so well in the splendid exhibition catalogue. But he loved and delighted in the Bushes and Shrubs.

Since they were less known or unknown, they gave him the excitement of discovery, and the opportunity to describe them to the world of books and bibliography. After Philip had explored a subject that had been neglected in the past, it would often assume a new importance to a wider circle of collectors. In this way Philip turned many Bushes *into* Oaks. For example: seventeenth-century Baroque illustrated books, Italian books of the eighteenth century, Edward Lear, Thomas Shotter Boys, Japanese calligraphy — all were areas of collecting in which Philip Hofer was a real pioneer.

The collecting of incunabula is a case in point: when Philip came to the Harvard Library in 1928, incunabula had been for over 150 years a top priority for book collectors, and they had been carefully studied by scholars since the middle of the nineteenth century. Great and erudite bibliographies had been compiled, especially in Great Britain and Germany. Harvard owned then almost 3000 incunabula — just about ten percent of those held by all American libraries. (In this very room the walls are normally lined with Harvard's great collection of incunabula — books printed earlier than 1501 — and now at last, to be the subject of a grand comprehensive catalogue by James Walsh.) Incunabula therefore was not a field to offer Philip much adventure and discovery, though over the years he acquired over a hundred examples of the choicest artistic quality — some given to Harvard during his lifetime, and the rest given now in this bequest — books such as the Naples Tuppo Aesop of 1485 and the great Dürer Apocalypse of 1498. Philip never set out in a deliberate *a priori* way to make a collection. An excitement would develop for a few books — and then he was off and running, building a great cluster which often became a definitive collection:

Baroque Illustrated Books
16th-Century French, Italian, German and Spanish
   Illustrated Books
The Artist and the Book — *livres de peintre* from 1860
   to today
Calligraphy and Calligraphic Manuscripts
Drawings for Books
Italian 18th-Century Illustrated Books
Press Books and Fine Printing over the last 100 years
Photography
Bibliography, especially with the provenance of great
   bibliographers and collectors
Edward Lear and Thomas Shotter Boys

There were clusters within clusters; for example, the many Holbein Dance of Death editions within the great collection of German sixteenth-century books. All these are in the Houghton Library. In the Harvard University Art Museums, to which Philip was very close, are his collections of:

Master Drawings
Albums of Prints by Lautrec, Piranesi, Redon,
   Vuillard and many others
Japanese Calligraphy and Illustrated Books

Many great manuscripts and drawings were given to his family, and certain drawings and rarities of photography were sold over the years, when his interest shifted to other pursuits.

In all these areas he opened up new paths and made new discoveries. In the French sixteenth century, where other collectors such as Charles Fairfax Murray concentrated on the early decades, with their mediaeval romances printed in gothic type, Philip saw the beauty of the books illustrated by the artists of the middle of the century, the Fontainebleau school — Jean Cousin, Jean Goujon, Bernard Salomon, René Boyvin — artists often influenced by Rosso and Primaticcio. These books were printed in roman type, with a typographic mastery never surpassed. He especially admired the architecture and perspective books of this period.

Baroque books, strangely neglected in the past, were Philip's own discovery, and the subject of his earliest important pioneering publication. His friendly rival, Lessing Rosenwald, considered these seventeenth-century illustrated books weak in typography and often too large in size. Philip loved the harmonious books of the sixteenth and eighteenth centuries, but he knew that there were other criteria that made other approaches worthy. The seventeenth century, the century of Descartes, Galileo, Spinoza and Newton produced books with illustrations by Callot, Rubens, Rembrandt and Della Bella, and Philip collected such books avidly.

Another discovery was the Rococo book of the Italian eighteenth century, especially the Venetian. Albums of prints were reasonably well known, though much remained to be discovered in the works of Piranesi and Bibiena, but the charming illustrated books, with their fanciful ornamental borders, contained in charming decorated paper bindings, were a special enthusiasm of Philip's.

Calligraphy and typography were, in a way, his first and *most* consistent love. It is interesting to note that he gave very little calligraphy or typography to Harvard during his lifetime, but retained such books and manuscripts until this final bequest.

Philip never sought completeness in any area of collecting. He aimed only for quality. He knew that completeness, while fun in a way, forced one to buy trivia in order to fill a so-called "gap." He looked down on people who made lists of the "100 Best" of this or that. With the exception of seventy Spanish books purchased from James Lyell, he never bought another person's collection intact and was particularly proud of this.

He didn't like everything. Seeing the tremendous scope of his collection, it would be hard for an outsider to grasp this quickly. He loved calligraphy, architecture and ornament, fable and emblem books — the sixteenth century was a special favorite. Just as the walls of *this* room are usually filled with Harvard's fifteenth-century books, the Reading Room of the Department of Printing and Graphic Arts displays on its shelves Philip's great sixteenth-century collections.

He was not enthusiastic about costume books and lace books, though he admitted there were a few exciting ones. He had an off-and-on relationship with festival books — Rubens' great book on the entry of the Archduke Ferdinand into Antwerp in 1635 was among his favorites. Many others he found boring.

Philip did not collect bindings if the book contained therein was of little interest. But — and his eyes would gleam — "what we want is a great book, in a great binding, with a great provenance (and of course in splendid condition)."

As to influences on Philip's collecting: first and foremost was William Ivins, the great curator of the Metropolitan Museum's Print Room in the 1920s through the 1940s — both Ivins in person, and through Ivins' writings. Only two print rooms in this country have *with* their prints a comprehensive collection of illustrated books — the Metropolitan Museum and the Museum of Fine Arts, Boston. This joining of prints and illustrated books is a natural one, since prior to the last hundred years or so, all books *had* to be illustrated with original prints (woodcuts, engravings, etchings and later on lithographs). There are probably as many original prints *in* books as exist separately. A reading of William Ivins' *Prints and Books* published by the Harvard University Press in 1926 will give some insight into the formative period of Philip's collecting taste. This book, to use a theological term, "prefigures" the Department of Printing and Graphic Arts.

Philip's daily work was enriched by his Harvard associates on both sides of Quincy Street. At the Fogg, the art historians and curators: Paul Sachs, Jacob Rosenberg, Agnes Mongan, Cary Welch, Max Loehr and John Rosenfield. And most of all, his colleagues at Houghton — Bill Jackson, Bill Bond, Roger Stoddard, Rodney Dennis, Jim Walsh, Kitzi Pantzer; and, in his own Department, Eleanor Garvey, the first Philip Hofer Curator, Peter Wick, Ruth Mortimer, David Becker, Roger Wieck, Anne Anninger and Nancy Finlay. The layout of the offices below couldn't be better for the interchange of ideas and opinions. At the opposite end of the corridor, the late Bill Jackson was often called on to discuss matters of bibliography, binding and provenance. Their relationship could be stormy at times, especially when Philip wished to dispose of a book (still in his own collection) which was not strongly visual, but pertinent to other Houghton collections. Newton's *Principia* was a case in point.

Philip had a tremendous influence on collectors and curators. It was not necessarily that he got them started, or even that he collected in their field. What he brought to them was his infectious enthusiasm, a lively interest in *their* ideas, and his amazing eye for quality in any area of the arts. He was always an *amateur*, in the true sense of the word.

I mention three well-known curators who were very much influenced by their association and friendship with Philip: Eleanor Sayre, preeminent Goya scholar and Senior Curator at the Museum of Fine Arts, Boston; Andrew Robison, outstanding expert on the work of Piranesi, the Curator of Prints and Drawings at the National Gallery; and Stuart

Cary Welch, Curator at the Fogg and Metropolitan Museum (as well as a private collector) of Indian and Islamic Art.

The list of collectors who shared their enthusiasms with Philip and saw him often and regularly is very long. To mention only a few — Francis Lothrop, Charles Mason, David Wheatland, Albert Lownes, Mary and Donald Hyde, William Bentinck-Smith, Edith Welch, W.G. Russell Allen, Peter Wick, David Becker, Charlotte and myself.

He had a wide circle of collector friends at the two clubs devoted to books, the Grolier Club (which he joined in 1924), and the Club of Odd Volumes (joined in 1931). Philip Hofer's interest in, and encouragement of, young book collectors was legendary. And in return, his association with these younger people seemed to keep him young in spirit, right to the end.

While Harvard was certainly the center of Philip's intellectual life in books and the arts, it was by no means the only institution which had the benefit of his energetic participation and support. There were also the Museum of Fine Arts, Boston, which he served as trustee for many years and as chairman of the committee to visit the Department of Prints and Drawings; the Boston Athenaeum, where he was a long-time trustee; and the Peabody Museum of Salem where he was an honorary curator; also the Smith College Museum, the Morgan Library, the National Gallery, and the Institute of Contemporary Art in its early days enjoyed his support.

In the last analysis, I think that Philip Hofer's collecting was shaped most of all by being in the context of Harvard. The late Gordon Ray, a friend of many of us in this room, once wrote that the future of rare book collecting might be in the hands of private collectors, or with institutions specializing only in books, such as the Huntington Library, because rare book collecting was really not a university's first priority. Although Philip often complained about this (in fact he complained a lot), and tended at times to agree with

Gordon Ray's thought, he realized very well that the best use of his books would be at the University. If the Houghton Library were located at a beautiful site on Philip's beloved Maine coast, it would still have its great collections. But with Houghton located as it is, attached by a bridge to the Widener Library and its three million books, and across the street from the great Fogg Fine Arts Library, the possibilities for the creative use of Philip Hofer's collections are without limit.   A.V.

Designed by Larry Webster
and printed in an edition of
1000 copies by Thomas Todd Company.
Cover adapted from a bookplate
by Stephen Harvard.